Accountability in
American Education:
A Critique

Accountability in American Education:

A Critique

Don T. Martin
University of Pittsburgh

George E. Overholt
Georgia State University

Wayne J. Urban
Georgia State University

PRINCETON BOOK COMPANY, *Publishers*
Princeton, New Jersey

Contents

We dedicate this book to our children:
Bill, Holly, Jennifer, Joe, Kristen, and Leslie

Preface

In the beginning of the 1970s it became apparent to most of us in the field of education that a "new" movement was rapidly emerging. Although books challenging educational practice such as *Crisis in the Classroom* were being widely discussed and the writings of the romantic critics advocating the open classroom were peaking, quieter but no less serious voices were being heard more frequently on the educational scene. It seemed as though this latter group had conceived of their theories in such a way as to oppose those of the free schoolers. Regardless of their original intentions, the theoretical framework of the new accountability proponents became antithetical to open education.

Severe budget problems were commonplace on the state and local levels during this period, which resulted in the adoption of austere fiscal policies by school budget planners. Moreover, this fiscal crisis caused legislators to eagerly search for new ways to cut the burgeoning costs of social services, especially those of education. The cost-cutting promises of the various accountability schemes then being proposed were undoubtedly attractive to the politicians seeking such economies. These same lawmakers began to enact state laws mandating accountability programs in state educational institutions, particularly those involved with teacher training.

The authors have been directly affected by this kind of political action. Each of us has been called upon to participate in accountability schemes in teacher training institutions which has given us direct knowledge about accountability practices. It is from these practices and our broad theoretical knowledge of accountability that our basic analysis is derived.

While doing the research for this book, we soon discovered a plethora of written materials favoring accountability and a paucity of critical writing. After thorough examination of the more important issues in accountability, we came to the conclusion that it was necessary not to write another favorable work but to write a critique; to do otherwise would have made a travesty of our intellectual and professional integrity.

Although written especially for students and colleagues in foundations of education, this book could be beneficial to all educators. The potential effects of accountability can be far-reaching and the general public, as well, could profit from an examination of its theoretical basis. Wherever used, this work, we believe, will generate controversy and subsequent discussion.

Few issues in education are as important and require more study today. Accountability programs are proliferating throughout the country and are often being implemented without critical or theoretical examination. It is hoped that this book will shed light on the central issues of accountability and in some way contribute to a more rational solution to the most pressing problems in American education.

The primary reason we are writing this book is to counter the all-inclusive claim made by many accountability advocates that their approach should be the only one to education. We are not opposed to accountability as one of many ways to solve our educational problems. We do challenge, however, the insistence of a single, universal approach to education, regardless of its theoretical or philosophical basis. To equate the basic theories of accountability with education is inaccurate, for any exclusive approach rules out those many features of learning which most men have held to be necessary to the concept of education.

Acknowledgment is made to Robert Morgart, Oakland University, for his contributions to the ideas on the political economy of accountability and to the American Federation of Teachers whose Educational Research for Action Grant supported the original research of the historical section. In addition, some of the central concepts in this book, in one form or another, were scrutinized by colleagues when presented as formal papers at national conventions, such as those of the American Educational Studies Association, the History of Education Society, and the Philosophy of Education Society.

D. T. M.
G. E. O.
W. J. U.
January, 1976

Accountability in
American Education:
A Critique

I

Introduction:
The Problem of Accountability

The loose rubric of "accountability in education" stands for both a movement and a cluster of associated ideas being currently recommended for use in schools. Among these ideas are, for example, the notion that all or most educational objectives should be couched in behavioral terms, the requirement that pedagogy be competence- or performance-based, the insistence on a strategy of educational evaluation which limits itself to that which can be observed and measured, and a call for the use of techniques of behavioral control which depend on an assumed instrumental relationship between means (generic behaviors) and ends (behavioral objectives). These and associated ideas stem from the nineteenth century positivism of Auguste Comte and Ernst Mach, and the twentieth century logical positivism of the "Oxford" school of philosophy. Among the leading proponents of this school of thought are Ludwig Wittgenstein, G. E. Moore, Gilbert Ryle, and A. J. Ayer.

Despite their differences, both the nineteenth and the twentieth century forms of positivism insisted on science as the only mode of knowledge. Classical problems of epistemology (theory of knowledge) were swept under the rug by appeal to an alleged scientific consensus of observation. Metaphysics was relegated to the dustbin of the meaningless and unintelligible because it could not be tested by observable experience.

Experience itself was "operationalized" to such an extent that it came to be represented only by a narrow domain of sense data. This shifted the emphasis from an attempt to "understand" things to an attempt to measure them. As a result, positivists proclaimed that insight, introspection, and creativity belonged only in subjective psychology, and not in science, logic, or philosophy. It was in this context that psychology became behaviorized. By concentrating on overt behavior, some psychologists committed themselves to the task of exorcising subjectivity from their discipline in hopes of establishing a "public" psychology analogous in its paradigms to that of the natural sciences.

On the other hand, natural scientists—especially since Einstein, Heisenberg, and Schrödinger—were engaged in the process of discovery. They freely accepted insight, they engaged in introspection, and they were creative. As a result, few modern natural scientists, and almost no physicists, accept the positivist view of science. They stress that an analysis of science which limits true statements to those which can be proved to correspond to what is observed and meaningful statements to those whose logical validity can be demonstrated admits either too little or too much. It admits too little in that all concepts not derived directly from experience are excluded—and this distorts the historical nature of science because it excludes much of what scientists have actually done.

Yet at the same time positivism admits too much when it extends the principle of verification to include those theoretical constructs of science which had been excluded by the more strict criteria, readmitting, for example, the metaphysics which the principle of verification originally had been designed to exclude. The principle of verification was invalidated—not, however, because it had been designed, at least in part, to exclude metaphysics, but rather because it could not provide an adequate account of science.[1]

These recent developments in the analysis of scientific theories relate to two current controversies. First, doubts have emerged about the value of natural science itself as traditionally understood by the positivists. Far from being accepted as the only paradigm of knowledge, science is being increasingly challenged regarding its capacity to make true statements about the world and to translate these "truths" into technologies. Second, the nature of alternative modes of knowledge, particularly in the social sciences, is becoming increasingly important. Many practitioners in these fields no longer automatically look to natural science for their methodological guidelines. Having lost much of their faith in the positivist paradigms of the natural sciences, they are becoming increasingly aware of the need to rethink their own aims and methods.

Nevertheless, many education scholars seem to have remained unaware of recent developments. They have not recognized that the positivist view of science is merely an earlier historical phase in the development of science, not the present reality. School policy, long known for its tendency to lag years behind developments

[1] For well-known rejections of the positivist view in favor of alternative interpretations of science, see: Albert Einstein, *Essays in Science,* Feyerabend, Paul K. "An Attempt at a Realistic Interpretation of Experience." *Proceedings of Aristotelian Society: 58,* 1957–1958, p. 143.

in other areas of knowledge, is only now feeling the full impact of the late nineteenth and early twentieth century positivistic view. The impact of positivism is clearly exemplified in the statements of spokesmen for the accountability movement in American education. Operating on the basis of an outmoded view of science and a now largely discredited faith in what it can do, accountability proponents call for the restructuring of curricula, methods, and evaluation.

In this book we discuss the three major defects within the movement loosely referred to as *accountability in education*. First, it lacks an adequate theoretical base. Second, it lacks reassuring historical precedents. In fact, something very akin to accountability has been tried before and found wanting. Third, its political implications are not reassuring to those among us who value either individuality or democracy.

Finally, because we believe that education has something to do with rational and critical thinking, introspection, and creativity, we believe that any view which confines itself exclusively to observable phenomena leaves out something essential both to the practice of science and to the process of education. We shall discuss what seems the most probable fate of education in an age of accountability.

From our perspective, such a critique as ours is urgently needed and must be undertaken now because our traditional notions about the value of democracy and the value of the individual are ultimately at stake. It would indeed be ironic if historians, through the advantages of hindsight, would one day notice that the loss of these values in our schools had coincided with our bicentennial. Such is the tragi-comedy of our times, that, in a misguided search for security, order, and economy, we might well come to discredit the notions of democracy and individual freedom while engaged in the very process of celebrating them. After all, if technology leads to power not only over nature but also over men, it also leads to the power of some men over others.

II

The Theoretical Background:
Basic Assumptions of Accountability

The social sciences—primarily behaviorist psychology, functionalist sociology, and social anthropology—have had considerable influence upon "accountabilist" recommendations for education. Yet, behind both behaviorism and functionalism lies the positivist view of the natural sciences. During the late nineteenth and first half of the twentieth centuries social scientists tended to look almost automatically to the natural sciences for their theoretical and methodological guidelines. In turn, educators have come in recent years to look increasingly to the social sciences for theoretical and methodological guidance. The result has been the presentation of a number of prescriptions for educational theory and practice which clearly find their origins in the basic tenets of nineteenth century positivism. This is to say nothing of the positivist style in contemporary philosophy of science and philosophy of education.

Although there are important differences between and among behaviorists and functionalists, they share a number of positivist or quasi-positivist assumptions. Among these are

1. A belief in external forms of determinism (usually termed *environmental* by behaviorists and *cultural* by functionalists)

2. A belief that overt behavior is an observable, testable phenomenon which can be adequately "captured" by operational definitions and quantified

3. A faith not in the possibility but in the actuality of a stable, commonly shared observation language of behavior, combined with the notion that any behavior or nonbehavioral language which cannot be translated into this observation language can be dismissed as unscientific

4. A belief that society can be improved through behavioral science and technology

These assumptions are usually translated directly into pedagogical language by the advocates of accountability.

Assumption 1 becomes the proposition that learning can be adequately defined as *change of behavior*. Thus learning becomes a behavioral process determined by external elements of the environment. It matters little to the argument whether these determinants are conceived as contingencies of reinforcement, social norms, or cultural prescriptives.

Assumption 2 becomes the proposition that learning viewed as change of behavior has been rendered observable and thus testable through the observation and measurement of behavioral performances.

Assumption 3 translates into the proposition that all of the above should be stated in a common observation language. Therefore educational curricula should have clearly stated behavioral or competence- or performance-based objectives which properly entail both the content and the method of instruction. It also follows as a corollary that behavioral objectives provide the necessary normative criteria for a "scientific" evaluation of educational performances. The emphasis shifts from input to output defined as *overt performances.*

Assumption 4 is reflected in the notion that methods and curricula are to be related to behavioral or performance objectives as means relate to ends. With the correct methods and curricula, it is believed we can accomplish whatever we think we need to get done. The notions of external determinism, the transformation of behavior into a testable phenomenon, the insistence on an observational language of behavior, and the belief in behavioral science and technology as the means to improvement of society are all clearly consistent with each of the pedagogical prescriptions listed.

Taken together, these prescriptions for education generate a *reductio ad absurdum* form of argument. This argument exemplifies the reductive fallacy which claims that learning is "nothing but" what has been stipulated. Advocates of accountability make no attempt to take adequate account of rival hypotheses or to refute them properly and systematically. The reduction results in its own breed of radical empiricism.

FUNCTIONALISM, BEHAVIORISM, AND ACCOUNTABILITY

Behind their differences functionalists, behaviorists, and accountabilists all share a central reference to relations among actual, empirically given social phenomena—whether they be institutions, groups, roles, individuals, or component elements of behavior. These relationships are claimed to be either (1) directly observable or (2) capable of abstraction from observation through direct induction. Thus, when a functionalist uses the term *social structure,* a behaviorist talks about *contingencies of reinforcement,* or an accountabilist describes *learning,* all are referring directly and without mediation to the observed organization of a given social or behavioral state of affairs at a given time. As the pioneer social anthropologist A. R. Radcliffe-Brown (1952) put it, ". . . direct observation does reveal to us that . . . human beings are connected by a complex network of social relations." His fuller formulation of the concept reads as follows:

> Individual human beings . . . are connected by a definite set of social relations into an integrated whole. The continuity of the social structure, like that of an organic structure, is not destroyed by changes in the units. . . . The continuity of structure is maintained by the process of social life, which consists of the activities and interactions of the individual human beings and the organized groups into which they are united. The social life of the community is here defined as the functioning of the social structure. The function of any activity is the part it plays in the social life as a whole and therefore the contribution it makes to the maintenance of the structural continuity.

Radcliffe-Brown also stated that "My view of natural science is that it is the systematic investigation of the structure of the universe as it is revealed to us through our senses."

B. F. Skinner (1953) has argued that the business of

psychology is the study of the connections between stimulus and response. We need not wait upon the other life sciences to tell us what happens in the neurology or biology of the organism. And neither need we pay attention to the intervention of internal mental processes if they are conceived to operate independently of physical causes. Notions of independent consciousness are not relevant to a functional analysis, he tells us, primarily because they are not observable. He also claims that such notions are fictions. They have no observable referents; therefore, they can never intervene between stimulus and response. As a result, we should stop agitating ourselves with such concerns and get on with the study of the connections between stimulus and response. This is how Skinner (1975) tells us, we should study human behavior:

> . . . the problems we face are not found in men and women but in the world in which they live, especially in those social environments we call cultures. It is an important and promising shift in emphasis because, unlike the remote fastness of the so-called human spirit, the environment is within reach and we are learning how to change it.

Skinner (1965) also argues that:

> We are concerned, then, with the causes of human behavior. We want to know why men behave as they do. Any condition or event which can be shown to have an effect upon behavior must be taken into account. By discovering and analyzing these causes we can predict behavior; to the extent that we can manipulate them, we can control behavior.

And Professor Skinner gives us further insight into his view of science in the following passage:

The external variables of which behavior is a function provide for what may be called a causal or functional analysis. We undertake to predict and control the behavior of the individual organism. This is our "dependent variable"—the effect for which we are to find the cause. Our "independent variables"—the causes of behavior—are the external conditions of which behavior is a function. Relations between the two—the "cause-and-effect" relationships in behavior—are the laws of science. A synthesis of these laws expressed in quantitative terms yields a comprehensive picture of the organism as a behaving system.

Professor Skinner (1975) also claims that techniques derived from such an analysis have already led to the improved design of cultural practices, in programmed instructional materials, contingency management in the classroom, behavioral modification in psychotherapy and penology, and many other fields.

Consequently, the statements of leading spokesmen for accountability in education should come as no surprise. James Popham (1972), for example, has stated that

Judgments about the success of an instructional procedure are made exclusively on the basis of results, that is, the changes in learner behavior which emerge as a consequence of instruction. Only if the hoped-for changes in learner behavior have been attained is the instructional process considered effective. Only when such changes have not been attained is the process judged ineffective.

. . . Because the criterion by which the success of the instructional process will be judged must be measurable learner behavior, the outcomes-oriented educator cleaves exclusively to objectives amenable to measurement. Whether they are called performance objectives, behavioral goals, operational objectives, or some equivalent phrase, they must be capable of post instructional assessment.

THE REDUCTIVE FALLACY AND WHERE IT LEADS

This is *reductio ad absurdum* with a vengeance. It clearly requires that all concepts relevant to the definition and evaluation of learning be empirically based. They can be nothing more than abstractions from observed life processes. The job of the scientist, in this light, is to record observed regularities and arrange them into empirical generalizations. The job of the educator is to apply these concepts, in turn, to the construction and evaluation of instructional processes. In either case, only observed phenomena are real. All alternative views are excluded. And this is accomplished by fiat, not through adequate refutation. That is why we have chosen to use the adjective "radical" for this form of empiricism. In some cases, the adjective "dogmatic," we would suggest, might also apply.

Above all, for the functionalist, the behaviorist, and the accountabilist alike, there are no hidden principles or relations to be uncovered. These social scientists are not involved in the construction of explanations. On the contrary, they are involved in the construction and application of "how-to-do-it" descriptions. Restricted to

the observation of recurrent regularities and the classi-
fication of them, the models thus derived—no matter
how sophisticated or complex—do not contain within
them significant explanatory power. No analytical break
with the phenomena can be made. One is proscribed
from "going behind or beyond" the appearances of the
phenomena. There is no possibility of stripping away
outer layers of the appearances of behaviors in order to
disclose their inner natures, as is the case, for example,
in psychoanalysis. For, according to this view, learning
is "nothing but" the behaviors themselves as they can
be observed to change.

As a result, the social scientist is prohibited from a
critical analysis of social phenomena because he is pre-
vented from going beyond the task of describing and
measuring them. His efforts yield a description of the
actual, empirically given arrangements of a specific
social or behavioral state of affairs. The educator is restricted to rearranging these observations on the model
of a means-end relationship (the end being a set of stated
behaviors viewed as performances; the means, a sequence
of stated behaviors instrumental to the end). His success
or failure is judged exclusively on these criteria.

LEARNING AND BEHAVIOR

But these are blunt and sweeping arguments. Let us
look more closely at several of the basic assumptions
here identified.

One of these assumptions is that learning can be adequately defined as *change of behavior*. Now the connec-
tion between learning and the ability to do something
is not simply an empirical one, as this definition seems
on the face of it to require. We would not be willing

to call any change of behavior an instance of learning. One may limp now though he did not before because he has had surgery on his "trick" knee or has sprained his ankle. He may hallucinate because he has taken drugs. He may see the tops of many people's heads because he has grown taller than the average person. He may exhibit schizophrenic behavior, although he has not done so in the past, because he now has an enzyme imbalance. He may act sleepy (rub his eyes and yawn) because he has taken a sleeping pill. He may cease acting schizophrenically because he has taken the doctor's prescription. The definition breaks down on all these examples. All are behaviors, they are observable, and they are in the process of changing or have changed. But how could we say that anyone has learned to do any of these things? Clearly, we would not agree that such behaviors as these can be counted as learned behaviors, or as evidence of learning. The definition of learning as change of behavior thus stands badly in need of qualification. Not all changes of behavior can count as either learning or evidence of it.

Conversely, not all learning is change of behavior— at least, not if it is intended that the definition shall refer exclusively to overt observable behavior. After all, is it not possible for human beings to engage in learning processes without manifesting them overtly? One example might be the forming and use of concepts. If one looks at a billiard table and notes that one of the balls is white and all the rest are not, he has formed a judgment utilizing concepts. He may also make other judgments about cue sticks, striking motions, the impact of one ball on another, and so on with an eye to propelling particular balls into selected pockets. Few educators would deny he has formed judgments by relating concepts in accordance with the rules of the game. And most would be willing to agree that he has thereby come to possess some kind of knowledge. He knows how to do something (in a purely cognitive sense, of course). It seems clear that we would be willing to call the process of acquiring this knowledge (whatever it may have been) a learning process.

But does our observer need to play billiards before he can be said to have learned anything? We stress that one can acquire an ability without manifesting it in overt behavior. For example, he may be simply standing to one side watching the game while intermittently combing his hair and smoking cigarettes. In such a case, anything that could be observed about his behavior would be simply irrelevant to any billiard playing knowledge he may be acquiring or rehearsing at the time.

This example is not pure fiction. One of the authors has learned most of what he knows about how to play billiards exactly this way: by watching others play. Note he was not simply copying what he saw others do—some players were rather bad ones, and he learned to discriminate between good and bad examples. And he seldom manifested this learning process while he was engaged in it. On the other hand, he occasionally reflected his learning by making statements about the game or by actually participating in it. In so doing, perhaps he provided the accountabilist's "proof" of his learning. Yet the accountabilist seems to want to say that *all* his learning processes and abilities are identical with his overt performances. But that seems to be asking too much. It would be more accurate to say that a person's overt performances are manifestations or, better yet, results of his learning and judgment-making abilities.

There are a host of problems here. Certainly a person can exhibit one kind of ability while engaged in the process of learning or rehearsing another. Consequently, descriptions of hair combing and cigarette smoking behaviors would be extremely misleading in the case of someone who was in fact learning how to play billiards. When one behaves he may be exhibiting *past* rather than *present* learning. Thus, descriptions of behaviors can be ambiguous indicators of learning. At any given time the behavior one exhibits is not always indicative of the learning in which he is engaged. Conversely, at any given time, the learning in which one is engaged may have nothing to do with his overt behaviors.

Nonobservable Learning

Still another problem lies in the fact that learning which is never directly manifested in behavior may still indirectly affect that behavior. Again we can cite personal experience to illustrate our point. One of the authors, as a schoolboy, learned to add figures by the old method of arranging numerals in columns, adding the right column, carrying "ones" or "twos" over to the next column to the left, and so on. He memorized the rules of this procedure well enough to be able to maintain good grades in arithmetic, but he never really understood what he was doing. When he got an answer he never knew whether or not it was right. All he could do was check his answer against that provided by the teacher or the workbook answer sheet. When that was not possible, he could only repeat the procedure. If he did not get the same answer twice in a row, he would have to repeat the procedure again and yet again and rely on a sort of majority vote answer—the one he had gotten two-out-of-three or three-out-of-four times.

He also found it difficult to add numbers rapidly and accurately "in his head." He would imagine a blackboard and try to see the problem as though he were writing it down. But that process almost always broke down on long problems because he would forget some of the numerals or what he had "carried over." Since he did not understand what he was doing, he could neither prove the rightness of his answers to himself nor work without pencil and paper. Despite these drawbacks, however, he was sufficiently careful with the procedure to get the right answer most of the time, and could demonstrate the procedure on demand. Thus, he fulfilled all the behavioral requirements anyone could ask.

Then in seventh grade, something happened. While learning to work with algebraic equations he noticed that he could think of addition problems not in terms of columns of numerals but rather in terms of blocks or chunks of numerical quantity. Suddenly the problem of adding, for example, 632 and 349 became a simple process of "seeing" that $600 + 300 + 30 + 40 + 2 + 9$ equaled 981. Now he not only "saw" that 981 was the right answer but also understood why. And he could do it all "in his head." This new system was strikingly different from the one he had been taught, and he never told anyone about it. No teacher ever knew what had happened or, in fact, that anything had happened at all. The seventh grade teachers only looked at his algebraic performance. They never knew that he was doing sums differently or even that he was doing them more rapidly and accurately than he had done them in the past. They never realized he could do them without recourse to pencil and paper.

Surely no one would object to calling this discovery

a learning process which resulted in a new and different kind of ability. It was not merely a matter of refining or improving an old ability; it substituted one kind of ability for another. Yet none of this was, in fact, ever directly observed by anyone. Nor could it have been. The only overt manifestation of this particular learning was his improved ability to add. Nothing about the new way of doing it was revealed. From a behavioral perspective, this change looks like a refinement of an ability when it was in fact a substitution of one method for another.

WEAKNESSES IN THE ACCOUNTABILISTS' DEFINITION

So far we have argued that the definition of learning as *change of behavior* is inadequate. At this point, however, an accountabilist might object that it is not any change of behavior, but rather *specific planned* changes of behavior which count. Yet even these modifications do not help the definition. If we add the prefix "planned" to the definition, we still do not allow for learning which is not directly manifested in behavior and for which there is no necessary behavioral equivalent. Learning cannot be clearly, and certainly not exclusively, equated with movement, stimulus, response, event, or object—planned or not.

If we insist on such a definition, then, we can no longer use the term *learning* as we ordinarily do. What we have seems to be not so much a *definition of* as a *prescription for* learning. We are not being told that learning is change of behavior, even if planned. We have seen a number of instances in which that statement would be false. We are being told, rather, that we *ought* to regard learning as change of behavior. Presumably, we should accept that statement, not because it is true, but because it gives us something we can measure.

The proposition that only performances be taken as evidence of learning suffers from defects similar to those already mentioned. The term *performance,* or any of its equivalents, refers to both learning and the result of learning. As we have seen, it cannot be equated with learning and neither is it always an accurate indicator of learning. It is merely a prescription. We are being told that we ought to use performances as tests of learning despite the fact that performances as learning processes and performances as tests of learning have not been distinguished. But they ought to be distinguished! Surely test results are what count, not test performances.

The recommendation that we use performances as evidence of learning, presumably, is also based on the notion that performances are measurable. Yet we can only infer learning from performance. To equate the two because we can thus get measurable results not only begs the question, it also results in confusion. And all this confusion of definitions, referents, and use of terms indicates that there is no existent stable observation language of behavior. It even raises suspicions as to whether such an observation language is possible!

Neither can the argument for an observation language of behavior be saved by recourse to operational definitions. Operational definitions do not give meanings of terms. They stipulate how they are to be measured. That is, they describe the phenomena which shall be taken to stand as referents for terms with respect to how those phenomena are to be measured. Such statements are not definitions at all. They are prescriptions subject to the reductive fallacy; they equate the measurement of something with the thing being measured. For example, operational definitions of intelligence seldom have anything to say about intelligence as such. But they do have a great deal to say about how it is to be measured. Such so-called definitions are really specifications of test and measurement criteria. Despite the fact that the meaning of the term *intelligence* and the way it is to be measured are quite different, the operational definition equates the two and thus confuses meaning with methods of verification. Meanings need not be verified. Statements which give meanings are neither true nor false. They depend on the conventions of a given language, not on observed fact or the stipulations of researchers. Meaning is a prerequisite for verification, not the method for verifying.

Why, then, are operational definitions in such wide use? They seem to be used because the task of reducing all talk about education to an observation language is so difficult. Translating a concept into observation language is not merely a task of substituting clear behavioral terms for vague nonbehavioral terms. In fact, it is not a matter of substituting clear for unclear terms at all. It is rather a matter of reducing all talk about education to behavioral terms. Reduction does not constitute clarification. It merely narrows the domain of discourse while confusing meaning with measurement. The clarification is more apparent than real, resulting in part from the peculiar but misleading power of the operational definition to reduce concepts and terminologies to stipulations of measurement.

THE CONSERVATIVE CHARACTER OF ACCOUNTABILITY

Assumption 4, introduced earlier, asserts that behavioral science and technology are the means to the improvement of society. This notion leads to consideration of what the term *improvement* means to functionalist social scientists, behavioral psychologists, and account-abilist educators. A reading of the pertinent literature suggests that, to them, improvement of society means the refinement of its administration. Accordingly, two attitudes, (1) a conservative political bias and (2) a belief in the functional necessity of social inequality, can be seen to follow as corollaries.

Functional theory tells us, if we recall the words of Radcliffe-Brown previously quoted, that the function of any particular part of a social system is the contribution it makes toward integrating and maintaining the total system which it inhabits. Both the individual person and education are included within this generalization.

Functionalists hold that a social system has a unity which may be defined as a functional one, and they draw a biological analogy. Just as the various parts of the structure of a simple organism, when functioning properly, contribute to the health and survival of that organism, so do the various parts of a social system, when functioning properly, contribute to the health and maintenance of the social network as a whole.

As a result, once they are satisfied that the existing structure of a society has been adequately described and categorized, the vast majority of functionalists take the existing structure of any society as a given. This is not a logical necessity, for the functionalist is free to take some prescriptive theoretical structure as a model, and some have done so. But the majority do not. For this majority, their theory inescapably develops a clearly conservative bias because the facts they work with are inherent in the existing structure of society. *Function*

becomes broadly defined as almost anything which contributes to the maintenance of the social structure, while
dysfunction becomes defined as that which does not
contribute to such an end or which contributes to some
alternative end.

At this point in the analysis, a clear teleology emerges,
and its conservative nature hardly seems deniable. In
this light, the term *function* implies a positive and the
term *dysfunction,* a negative or pejorative judgment.
Anything defined as a dysfunction is seen as a situation
that needs to be remedied. It is exactly in this mode
that the functional social sciences most often become
"applied"—especially in education. Behavioral modification techniques provide a clear illustration. Mean-
while, that which is defined as functional implies a
situation which is to be maintained or perhaps rein-
forced. Both theory and practice, in this case, become
socially and politically conservative. We would have to
stretch the ordinary conventions of our language a long
way to call them anything else.

THE ELITIST CHARACTER OF ACCOUNTABILITY

Functionalist theory also involves the concept of social
inequality. Once again, such a view is not inherent in
the theory, and not all functionalists have adopted it.
Two conditions must obtain. First, the existing structure of society must be assumed as a given, thus supply-
ing the necessary conservative teleology. And, second, the
society in question must be one which is hierarchically
stratified. In such a case, it follows that the requirements
of maintaining the system lead to a view of social inequality as functional. That is, the stratification of

persons becomes a functional necessity. Those functionalists who have adopted this view, it is suggested here,
far outnumber those who have not. A clear example
of one who has embraced this view is the sociologist
Kingsley Davis (1949). On this subject he states:

> If the rights and prerequisites of different positions
> in a society must be unequal, then the society must
> be stratified, because that is precisely what stratifi
> cation means. Social inequality is thus an uncon
> sciously evolved device by which societies insure
> that the most important positions are conscien
> tiously filled by the most qualified persons. Hence
> every society, no matter how simple or complex,
> must differentiate persons in terms of both prestige
> and esteem and must therefore possess a certain
> amount of institutionalized inequality.

Now the functionalist, or indeed the educator, who
has traversed this path from empiricism through conservatism to social inequality has most certainly come
a far way from scientific objectivity. As Irving L. Horowitz (1968) has argued in reference to Davis, there are
directly conservative political judgments involved in
this view. And also, one suspects, a hint of elitism. Yet
adherents of such views usually claim that they are free
of such extraneous value judgments. They claim to be
"scientific."

Nevertheless, it is difficult to see how Davis, or anyone
else for that matter, can present an explanation of social
stratification as a functional necessity and fail to recognize that such a view constitutes one of the cornerstones
of conservative political theory. Davis' functional neces-

sity emerges as a defense of the *status quo* in a stratified society. He has the right, if it is his conviction, to present and argue for such a view. But he does not have the right, as Horowitz has so ably pointed out, to claim that there is a scientific or sociological mandate for such a view.

RADICAL EMPIRICISM, SYSTEM MAINTENANCE,
AND SOCIAL INEQUALITY

Education must be critically involved in whatever social theory that is prevalent so long as it is to remain a viable social institution. In modern society, education has tended to become locked into a network which includes science, technology, industry, and government. This network, upon which much of education's support has come to depend, tends to be dominated by societal views, and especially by the four assumptions previously outlined. The current popularity of systems analysis provides an excellent example. Thus, within our societal network, the relation of education to life has become increasingly defined in behavioral terms; that is, as the application of empirically derived and legitimated techniques for maintaining the total network. The reductive fallacy involved in all this thinking is neglected. And the result of such neglect is that the social potential of education is becoming replaced by the social potential of behavioral control. The function of schooling becomes increasingly defined as the production and administration of processes of technical control. Education as an agent of enlightenment leading to individual autonomy is seldom considered any more. Its place has been taken by behavioral research which concentrates almost exclusively on the production of technological recommendations supportive of the network defined *status quo*.

Such efforts contribute little to the abilities of students or educators to understand themselves or to envision what might be as opposed to what is. In other words, *enlightenment* is an adjective which no longer describes anything considered to be very real, important, or functional about the relationship between school and life. Its place has been taken by terms like *performance* or *competency based,* which describe attempts to attain control over objective or objectified process and persons. The basic assumptions have become radical empiricism, system maintenance, and social inequality. It is in these assumptions and the practices that flow from them that accountabilists' views of schooling and its benefits may be distinguished from other ways of conceiving what education is and what it is good for.

As a result, a school policy dominated by the accountabilist's view cannot direct itself toward individuals who communicate with each other to share their mutual concerns. Rather, it is directed toward the behavior of human beings who manipulate or are manipulated. As such, an accountabilist pedagogy can refine the organization and administration of life, but it cannot transcend it. It contains no critical dimensions; it lacks the capacity for self-criticism or self-correction. The accountabilist's policy can administer modes of behavior in terms of some given societal model (usually the view dominant in the network), but it can make no move toward any higher, better, or more enlightened state of affairs.

In short, an accountabilist pedagogy imposes arbitrary limitations on human potential. For example, it makes no attempt to help obtain (or to develop students' abilities to obtain) a rational consensus concerning the control of their individual and collective fates. Little Johnny becomes, himself, an objectified part of the attempt to improve society by constantly refining its administration. In the last analysis, an accountabilist pedagogy offers him only two roles: that of the administrator or that of the administrated, that of the manipulator or that of the manipulated. The drive for enlightenment, by contrast, relates education to political life. Indeed, it strives for a particular conception of political life—a democratic one—by contributing to the possibility of rational consensus through shared modes of communication, meaning, and concern. Through such a perspective, human beings can join together into collectives capable of taking socially significant action. Individuals and groups which can act in their own behalf in turn may rekindle the possibility of critique and reform.

An accountabilist pedagogy, on the other hand, constitutes one of the first lines of defense against precisely such a contingency. It incorporates assumptions which lead people to mistake social control for social action and thus to replace social action with refined means of control. Through the filter of these assumptions, terms, and definitions we are led to see society as a matrix of behavioral regularities, each of which may be positively or negatively judged in terms of the requirements of system maintenance. What we are left with is the rather dreary prospect of a society in which any kind of coherent consensus based on the powers and actions of individuals who are rational, politically enlightened, and disposed to act within a moral dimension becomes continuously less possible. In this way the possibility of democracy itself continuously recedes not only from our grasp but even from our view.

REFERENCES

Davis, Kingsley. 1949. *Human Society.* New York: Macmillan.

Horowitz, Irving L. 1968. *Professing Sociology.* Chicago: Aldine Publishing Company.

Popham, James W. 1972. Focus on Outcomes: A Guiding Theme of E. S. '70 Schools, in Arthur Olson and Joseph Richardson (eds.), *Accountability: Curricular Applications.* Scranton, Pa.: Intext Publishers.

Radcliffe-Brown, A. R. 1952. *Structure and Function in Primitive Society.* London: Cohen and West.

Skinner, B. F. 1953. *Science and Human Behavior.* New York: Macmillan.

——. 1965. *The Science of Behavior.* New York: Macmillan.

——. 1975. The Steep and Thorny Way to a Science of Behavior, reprinted from Rom Harre (ed.), *Problems of Scientific Revolution,* The Herbert Spencer Lecture Series, 1973. Reprinted by permission of The Clarendon Press, Oxford, *American Psychologist,* January, 1975, p. 49.

III

The Historical and Contemporary Foundations of Accountability

As may be discerned from the previous chapters, there is much confusion over the term *accountability,* and numerous attempts have been made to define it.[1] The confusion stems from the way accountability has become intertwined with concepts like behavioral objectives, performance contracting, achievement testing, and competency based education, all of which have in common their ability to be measured "objectively"—that is by standardized, quantitative techniques. Indeed, a major component of any definition of accountability lies in its insistence on framing educational results in measurable terms.

At least two major objections have been raised to the notion that educational results should be framed in measurable terms. The first is that such a notion leads to a narrow definition of education where whatever

[1] The literature on accountability is extensive. Almost any issue of the *Phi Delta Kappan* for the years 1971–1973 contains one or more articles on accountability. Gene V. Glass, "The Many Faces of 'Educational Accountability,'" *Phi Delta Kappan,* LIII (June, 1972), 636–639, contains a lucid discussion of the various meanings of *accountability.*

cannot be measured is ignored.[2] A curriculum that is devoted only to measurables may well ignore areas that emphasize thought processes or aesthetic qualities which are difficult or impossible to measure. The fact that they are difficult to measure does not mean that they are unimportant; yet accountability, in relying on objective measures, implies that nonmeasurables do not count.

The second objection to standardized measures in accountability systems is that while measures may distinguish between those pupils who have learned something and those who have not, they say nothing about how or why the learning did or did not take place. This is where accountability goes beyond objective measurement: it infers, from measurable results, judgments about who or what is responsible for those results. As one authority in the measurement field put it: ". . . there is no realistic hope for validly attributing this or that group of pupils' ignorance or competence to a particular teacher or school." (Glass, 1972) Yet most accountability systems try to do precisely that; they make the teacher or group of teachers responsible (accountable) for the pupil's success or failure in school.

Accountability, then, is a system for rewarding teachers according to their pupils' performance on some standardized measures of learning. And yet, as many educators stress, these standardized measures are paradoxically incomplete or invalid as a basis for evaluating teachers.

[2] A critique of behavioral objectives which emphasizes the sterility of relying on only measurables can be found in William E. Doll, "A Methodology of Experience: An Alternative to Behavioral Objectives," *Educational Theory*, XXII (Summer, 1972), 309–324.

The objections are formidable, but they do not seem to have blunted the movement toward accountability.[3] Why is this so? One explanation for the failure of accountability advocates to heed objections by educators is that accountability is not primarily a pedagogical movement. It is an administrative system, and as such it is impervious to arguments which are based on educational concerns. Accountability works administratively; that is, it does present a way of rewarding certain activities and punishing others.

If, then, accountability does not respond to educators, to whom or what does it respond? Answering this question brings us to a consideration of the second term to be elaborated, the *foundations* of accountability. By *foundations,* we mean those factors in the larger society which help to explain what goes on in schools. These factors may be political, social, and/or economic. The popularity of the current accountability movement, despite the objections of educators, seems related to both a political and an economic concern. These concerns are voiced in Leon Lessinger's (1970) *Every Kid a Winner,* a book we might call the Bible of the accountability movement.

In his first chapter, Lessinger, speaking from years of experience as an administrator, invokes the right of students to learn and the right of taxpayers to know what results education produces in return for the dollars spent on it. The right of students to learn has a two-fold thrust: to counteract the danger of schools' not teaching all children basic skills such as reading and writing, and

[3] The objections to accountability are well presented in Allan C. Ornstein and Harriet Talmage, "The Rhetoric and the Realities Accountability," *Today's Education,* LXII (September–October, 1973), 70–80.

to highlight the political powerlessness of low-income parents whose children are the ones who most often fail to learn. Lessinger implies that the teacher or the school, once it knows that it is responsible for learning, will bring about that learning. This is, as we have seen, a highly tenuous conclusion. Yet even if Lessinger's accountability cannot improve learning it can accomplish a political purpose by penalizing teachers—thereby appearing to make the school responsive to the rising political consciousness in the low-income areas of our urban centers.

The economic aspect of the accountability movement relates to the right of the taxpayer to know the results of the expenditures on education. This, for Lessinger, means that learning must be linked to its costs. Consequently, learning must be stated in quantifiable terms which are then related to cost statements. This economic quantification reflects the increasing societal concern over the amount of money spent on education. This concern, which has been voiced strongly since the last few years of the 1960s, is rooted in several factors which we hope to uncover in this chapter.

The strength of the concern over educational expenditures seems especially surprising because it follows closely on the heels of the Great Society era in which expenditures for education were plentiful. Yet the history of public education, both in this country and abroad, reveals that concern over educational expenditures is the rule, not the exception. Let us look briefly at two episodes in the history of public education, the first in nineteenth century England and the second in early twentieth century America. These historical examples will demonstrate that accountability is not a new movement; indeed, comparable movements have arisen in response to similar political and economic events.

Our historical treatment should enable us to return to a consideration of the contemporary situation with a fuller perspective and to discuss more clearly the current accountability movement, the political and economic forces to which it is responding, and possible alternatives to it.

ACCOUNTABILITY IN NINETEENTH CENTURY ENGLAND

English schooling in the mid-nineteenth century was administered under a system known as "payment by results." This system has been described recently by Jeanette B. Coltham and Alan A. Small (1972), both of whom noted the parallels in payment by results and accountability between then and now. The payment-by-results system involved the examination of elementary school students by state school inspectors. The inspectors gave the same standard examination to each child. Funds were then appropriated to each school on the basis of its students' scores on the examinations.

Both Coltham and Small note that one result of the system of payment by results was a considerable narrowing of the curriculum. The 3 R's, being the subjects measured by the inspectors, became the most important school subjects. Subjects such as geography and history ". . . were frequently dropped to provide more time for repeated drill on the examinable material." Matthew Arnold, in 1867 a school inspector in England, commented that students who passed the tests in reading, writing, and ciphering did not necessarily possess the skills supposedly being measured. He also noted that payment by results yielded a mechanical turn that was trying to the intellectual life of the school. Coltham compared the deadly mechanical teaching in the elementary schools, which functioned under "payment by results," to the teaching in infant schools where teachers were not evaluated by student examination. According to Coltham's reading of inspectors' reports, teachers in primary schools ". . . find greater freedom to decide for themselves how and what children should be taught, and they were willing and able . . . to use the ideas of such educators as Pestalozzi, Froebel, Dewey, and Montessori. . . ." For Coltham and Small, who rely on nineteenth century authorities for evaluation, payment by results was an educational disaster. Yet their criticisms of the English system are similar to those of the contemporary critics of accountability discussed earlier in this chapter.

The English experiment continued several years, despite the opposition of educators. Its longevity stemmed from political and economic factors which influenced decision makers more than the objections of teachers or school inspectors. England, at the time the payment-by-results system was used, had the most highly industrialized society in the world. As the industrial revolution spread throughout the country, factories sprang up in city after city, and the harsh poverty of factory workers and the unemployed became more and more visible. Educating the children of these urban poor people was seen as necessary by both humanitarians, genuinely interested in uplifting the poor, and by others more concerned with preventing a revolution. Working people themselves often desired education for their children as a means to social and economic mobility.[4]

[4] For a study of the support of education by the working classes in England during this period, see Brian Simon, *Studies in the History of Education 1780–1870* (London: Lawrence & Wishart, 1960).

In response to these pressures, the amount spent by the English government for schooling increased significantly during the 1840s and 1850s. In fact, during the 1850s the government increased its financial support about 100,000 pounds annually. The combination of the variously motivated concerns for the education of the poor and the anxiety generated by the increase in state expenditures for education resulted in a Royal Commission to investigate the state of Popular Education in England and to consider and report what Measures, if any, were required for the extension of sound and cheap elementary instruction to all classes of the people.

The call for "sound and cheap" elementary instruction was answered by legislation, passed by Parliament during 1862, known as the Revised Code. This was the legislation that produced payment by results, the nineteenth century English accountability system. The juxtaposition of the adjectives "sound and cheap" indicates the existence of both an educational and an economic concern in the minds of the sponsors of this educational experiment. Advocates of this system thought that educational soundness and cheapness could and would go together. Yet by far the most important outcome of the payment-by-results system was the reduction of government expenditures for education, the amount decreasing from 813,441 pounds in 1861 to 76,000 pounds in 1865.

The English government, in enacting payment by results, reflected the desires of those groups who sought controlled spending on education for the poor. Government policy reduced the amount spent on education while at the same time promising but failing to deliver better education. Small goes so far as to suggest that payment by results was a kind of upper-class plot involving those ". . . who hate and fear the education of the lower classes and therefore give their support to a plan which will guarantee that the poor get no instruction beyond the bare minimum in the 3 R's." Clearly, in the English experiment the educational considerations became secondary to political and economic considerations.

The opposition to the English payment-by-results system which arose at the time of its introduction was particularly interesting. Teachers provided the bulk of the resistance, and they based their objections on both educational and economic grounds. As mentioned before, they abhorred the narrowness and mechanical character the system imposed on the educational process. They also objected to the economic burden forced upon them by basing their pay on student performance. Teacher opposition to this system continued throughout the remainder of the nineteenth century; but it was not until very late in the century, when the teachers organized themselves into the National Union of Elementary Teachers and other groups such as the Froebel Society, that they were able to help end the system of payment by results.

ACCOUNTABILITY IN EARLY TWENTIETH CENTURY AMERICA

If we turn our attention now to the American scene in the early years of the twentieth century and the trend in educational administration known as the *efficiency movement*, we find a situation analogous to both nineteenth century England and contemporary conditions. This movement has been described and evaluated quite thoroughly by Raymond E. Callahan (1962), who saw efficiency as a "cult" used by the developing profession of educational administration to retain its foothold in the schools. Efficiency, as described by Callahan, promised a dual outcome similar to that provided by payment by results. Efficient administration would provide both a better and a less expensive education; it would be both "sound and cheap." Callahan copiously documents this dual promise by efficiency advocates.

For example, he cites the publication of Leonard Ayres' (1909) book *Laggards in the Schools*. Ayres examined school attendance and promotion figures and found that many students were dropping out of school. Still others were lagging behind their peers; they were not in the same grade level as their age mates, but rather in a grade with younger children. Ayres, instead of inquiring why these children were behind, simply labeled them "laggards," cited their grade placement as an example of educational inefficiency, and urged that the situation be remedied by cost accounting techniques such as those used by businesses and factories. When all students were at the normal grade level for their chronological age, school inefficiency would be remedied and proper educational output would be achieved.

This was, obviously, an extremely narrow view of the educational process. Indeed, Callahan noted the elevation of budgetary values over educational concerns. "Efficiency" promised that close attention to educational bookkeeping could solve the problems of students. Subjects that could not be kept in the books, such as music and art, were ignored by the efficiency advocates; those in which progress could be neatly and "scientifically" measured were stressed. Again, the narrowness of the advocates of efficiency seems similar to the 3 R's emphasis of the payment-by-results advocates and the current emphasis which accountability advocates place on areas which can be "objectively" measured.

Once more, strong political and economic forces influenced the movement for efficiency in education. First, efficiency was borrowed directly from business and industry. Efficiency in business, industry, and education typified the large middle-class reform thrust which swept the country during the first two decades of the twentieth century.[5] These efficiency reformers were reacting to the urbanization and industrialization which drastically changed the face of American society during this period. One particularly difficult problem which confronted the early twentieth century public schoolmen was the immigrant child. These children, who formed a sizable portion of those "laggards" discussed by Ayres, did not seem to respond to education as well as native children.[6] To develop special curricula or teaching strategies for them would have cost a great deal of money. Instead of trying to get and then spend this money, educational administrators employed efficient management as the solution.

One wonders what caused administrators to reason in such a blatantly irrational manner. Callahan attributes their actions to what he calls the "vulnerability" of school administrators. These men were vulnerable because their profession was in its infancy. "School

[5] Callahan describes the efficiency movement in general while Richard Hofstadter, *The Age of Reform: From Bryan to F.D.R.* (New York: Vintage Books, 1955), Chapter 4, discusses the middle-class aspect of the reform movements of this period.

[6] For the attitudes and policies of educators toward immigrants during this period, see Henry J. Parkinson, *The Imperfect Panacea: American Faith in Education, 1865–1965* (New York: Random House, 1968), Chapter 3.

administration" had not yet discovered any theoretical, educational rationale on which to base its claim for acceptance. Efficient management became a substitute for an educational rationale, and administrative professionals boasted of how they could save money and run the schools well.

Administrators also were dishearteningly vulnerable because they had to rely on lay boards of education for jobs and funds. These boards were dominated by businessmen and other representatives of the affluent groups in society whose choice—when confronted with a reform which might cost money or one which promised at the same time to solve whatever problem was ailing the system and to save the taxpayers' dollars—was obvious. School administrators were neither established enough as an occupational group nor in possession of a body of knowledge on which to build an alternative approach to education. Thus, they aided and abetted the cost-conscious school boards.

Opposition to the efficiency craze came from a few superintendents, a few leading educators such as John Dewey and William Bagley, and (most interestingly for our purposes) from teacher organizations. Callahan notes the opposition to efficiency voiced in the *American Teacher* in 1912:

> We have yielded to the arrogance of "big business men" and have accepted their criteria of efficiency at their own valuation, without question. We have consented to measure the results of educational efforts in terms of price and produce—the terms that prevail in the factory and department store. But education, since it deals in the first place with organisms, and in the second place with individualities, is not analogous to a standardizable manufac-

turing process. Education must measure its efficiency not in terms of so many promotions per dollars of expenditure, nor even in terms of so many student-hours per dollar of salary; it must measure its efficiency in terms of increased humanism, increased power to do, increased capacity to appreciate.

At about this time, Atlanta teachers organized their opposition to an efficiency-minded reform administration. In 1914, a new president of the board of education was named in Atlanta, and he proceeded to fire the incumbent superintendent, bring in a new man, and inaugurate a series of reforms. Each reform proposed and implemented by the board president resulted in some cut being made in teacher pay, either directly or through an increase in class size or work day without an accompanying pay raise. The local teachers' association moved deliberately, and, in 1918, participated in a city council investigation of the board which resulted in the resignation of the board president (Urban, 1973). Here, in addition to the pedagogical narrowness highlighted in the New York opposition to efficiency, we see how organized teachers in Atlanta viewed efficiency as a distinct economic threat to their well being. Organizations of teachers fought anti-efficiency battles in several other large cities, including Chicago. The dual concerns and the organized nature of the teacher opposition to the efficiency administrators parallel the opposition to payment by results in England.

HISTORICAL RELEVANCE TO THE CURRENT MOVEMENT

The step of relating one of our historical examples, the cult of efficiency described by Callahan, to the current accountability movement has been taken in a review of Leon Lessinger's book on accountability. Richard Olmsted (1972), in his review, compares the arguments of Lessinger to those of Franklin Bobbitt, one of the leaders of the efficiency movement. Direct parallels in the ideas of Lessinger and Bobbitt include (1) suggesting business as a model for educators to emulate, (2) emphasizing objective measures as the sole criterion for educational evaluation, and (3) promising both better education and cost control through sophisticated accounting procedures.

Though the two sets of ideas are not identical, their essential compatibility indicates that Lessinger, rather than developing a new or different system, has merely brought efficiency up-to-date. For example, the actual accounting procedures are different in the two plans, but this shift reflects the changes in accounting procedures without negating the important similarity of the continued faith in business procedures as a solution to educational problems. Another difference in the two sets of ideas is the industry each man uses for his model. Bobbitt relied on the steel industry and its factories as his model, while Lessinger relies on the space industry. Each chose the type of industry which was glamorous in his period. More importantly, Lessinger's use of the space industry as a model allows him to give the federal government a sizable role in his system, a role that was unknown in the private enterprise world of the early 1900s.

Olmsted, while indicating in his review the relationship of accountability to economic developments external to education, ends his review with a recommendation which ignores the external forces. Both Callahan and Olmsted see the main deficiency of the movements they are describing as the narrowing and limiting of the educational process. Thus, they plead for a broader conception of the educational process. Unfortunately, in so doing, they have overlooked the most important part of their own analyses: that educational developments tend to reflect larger political and economic developments. Prescribing a strictly educational cure, as they both do, focuses on the symptoms rather than on the causes of the problem. If these movements in education are politically and economically derived, then a cure which ignores the source of the movement would be short-sighted and probably short-lived.

This point has been elegantly made by Martin Levit (1972) in an essay on the current accountability movement. He begins with the now familiar argument that accountability dangerously limits the range of formal school activities to those which are measurable. This type of program, which closes the educational universe, is called "scientific" by its advocates. Levit argues, however, that a truly scientific program would *expand* educational outcomes to include the abilities to inquire and add to knowledge as desirable educational goals. Levit supplements the familiar narrowness argument with the criticism that the accountability program is not scientifically grounded. Accountabilists offer a program for which they present no empirical evidence on which to base their claims. The accountabilists' appeal to science and empirical measurement is thus, for Levit, disingenuous.

Levit indicates that accountability might better be considered as a political and economic movement when he describes it as an ideology, a system of illusory ideas that perpetuates the existing social system by preventing education from serving all classes. This is the reality

despite the fact that the current accountability movement, like its historical predecessors, stresses "service
to the poor."

The promise of service to the poor in the current
accountability movement is emphasized in Lessinger's
title, *Every Kid a Winner,* as well as in his statement of
"the right of every child to learn." The weakness in this
approach, according to Levit, is that when it concentrates on narrow objectives and educational plans to
achieve them, it accepts the present social order as a
given. Accountability prevents analysis of the influence
of social and economic factors on school success by forc-
ing educators to concentrate on measuring and testing
learning in a social vacuum.

Accountabilists seem unwilling to consider that school
success is related to one's place in the economic class
structure of society, that internal educational issues are
related to external economic forces. This truism, which
has been uttered so often that one wonders how it can
be ignored, nevertheless is ignored by accountability
advocates. They prefer to tinker with educational reforms that studiously avoid the economic correlates of
learning. Levit ends his article by calling for an alternative to accountability which would involve a restructuring of the socioeducational system (his label for sig-
nifying the relationship of educational and economic
success). Levit has thus taken us not only beyond the
solutions of the accountabilists but also beyond the
statement of Callahan and Olmsted. Educational problems must be considered at their foundations, their
political and economic aspects, if they are to be dealt
with effectively. Levit indicates that this analysis will
be difficult and complex.

Despite the enormity and complexity of the task, we

intend to make a beginning at an analysis of the political and economic forces in the current accountability movement. Our historical examples provide us with material to make a comparative study. One consistent factor in the historical examples was the existence of economic and political power groups in the payment-by-results and efficiency camps. This situation is similar in the current accountability movement, but the complex structure of our own society makes the analysis more difficult.

Lessinger's space industry model, as already noted, invokes an industry in which the roles and inputs of government and private corporation are mixed. This is the prime characteristic of our modern economy. The conjunction and interpenetration of the interests of government and large corporations has been noted by several social scientists.[7] The line between the private and public sectors in our society has become blurred as private corporate capital has come to influence and control government at all levels in advanced industrial societies. The old desire of the small capitalist entrepreneur to keep government out of business has been replaced by the government's current role as the presumed regulator and often, as in the case of Penn Central and Lockheed, savior of big business. Lessinger's reliance on large corporations as educational consultants and evaluators and the federal government as a financer of accountability schemes is consistent with these current economic realities.

But why are the federal government and large corporations involved in the current accountability move-

---

[7] An early and famous explanation of this point was made by C. Wright Mills in his book *The Power Elite* (New York: Oxford University Press, 1956).

ment? The economist, James O'Connor (1970) gave one answer to this question in his article, "The Fiscal Crisis of the State." O'Connor's argument is so long and complex that we shall only outline it briefly here, emphasizing the parts of the argument which bear on the topic of accountability. The article begins with the now familiar point that our contemporary economic system, corporate capitalism, fuses the previously separated private economic and public political systems. This fusion causes the state (government at all levels) to undertake policies which directly enhance corporate profits and capital expansion. Examples of this kind of activity are government highway expenditures, urban renewal projects, and vocational education programs. The corporate beneficiaries of such public subsidies in these examples respectively are road contracting and construction companies, building contractors, and the corporate employers receiving the trained labor turned out by vocational education programs. Educational accountability schemes, which provide for evaluation of programs by "learning corporations" and for corporate performance contractors to design and carry out accountability programs, are other examples of state subsidies to corporate capital.

But the state, in subsidizing corporate capital, strains its own budget at the same time that public (state) employees, including teachers, are organizing to deal with their tightening economic situation. The fiscal crisis is inevitable. The state, while increasing expenditures that benefit corporate capital, has to deal with employees' demands for better wages and working conditions, all in the context of a taxpayer revolt.

The state can raise funds to meet its expenditures, according to O'Connor, only in three ways: (1) by engaging in profit making enterprises itself, (2) by expanding the number of state loans (thereby increasing the state debt), or (3) by increasing taxes. The first alternative, public ownership of a profit-making enterprise, is difficult in American society with its strong commitment to private profit-making enterprise. This ideological commitment to capitalism allows business to preserve, for itself, the direct profit-making activities.

The second alternative, state loans (through bond issues of all kinds) is becoming more and more difficult because of rising interest rates and increasing concern over government debt. The furor over large cities such as New York hovering near default provides a vivid example. To compound the problem, bond issues are allowed for financing public buildings but not for employee salaries. State payrolls have rapidly increased since the mid-1950s and no doubt they will continue to accelerate at a similar rate in the near future.

The elimination of the first two alternatives leaves taxation as the only viable way for the state to finance its expenditures. The heart of the fiscal crisis is that even this avenue has been closed by the taxpayers. They are revolting against tax increases of any kind—property, sales, income, etc. O'Connor sees this phenomenon as an eminently rational response by the taxpayer to the gross inequities in our tax structure. He indicates that every tax currently levied is regressive—even those presumably progressive taxes such as the corporate income tax, since corporations are allowed to pass the tax on to the consumer through higher prices.

The fiscal crisis, then, occurs when the state cannot raise the necessary funds. The crisis worsens when the state also cannot blunt the financial impact of public employee wage increases by increasing public employee productivity. Private industry can usually maintain or increase profits despite increasing worker wages by either passing the raise on to the consumer in the form of higher prices, or passing it back to the worker by increasing his productivity. Public employers, however, cannot easily use either of these strategies. The price for public services is ultimately controlled by voters, and most public employees provide services where their productivity is very difficult to measure.

This latter consideration, raising productivity, brings us to the source of the current educational accountability movement. Seen in the context of the fiscal crisis of the state, accountability is an attempt to raise the educators' productivity by evaluating education in ways that are measurable, though fallacious. This process effectively brings educational expenditures under the authority of the corporate financial interests which can increasingly be served either indirectly if a state apparatus does the evaluating, or more directly by a private evaluation process. In our contemporary situation, as in our historical examples, then, accountability is more of an economic and political issue than an educational issue.

Further, this interpretation explains how current accountabilists simply ignore the pedagogical objections to their systems. For example, former United States Commissioner of Education, Sidney P. Marland (1972) dealt with the arguments of those who stated that accountability leaves out that which cannot be measured in the following manner: "Nevertheless, the theory of accountability calls for us, if we establish such goals as 'the socialization of the child,' [Marland's example of an unmeasurable goal] to verbalize these goals in measurable terms, and we must seek ways to do so." The arguments of opponents are evidently to be pushed aside. Either an educational matter can be measured or it is not to exist. This may be the best evidence that the current movement is part of the larger state effort to control public budgets and has little or nothing to do with educational issues per se.

A RESPONSE TO ACCOUNTABILITY

The thesis which emerges from the foregoing analysis is that *accountability, both in its historical and contemporary forms, is an issue that has its roots in political and economic policies.* If the argument is correct and this is the case, how can educators deal with this politico-economic accountability movement? The first step might be to identify those groups within the larger body of educators who could be expected to support the movement. Callahan's argument of the vulnerability of school administrators to efficiency influences seems to be valid also for the contemporary situation. Callahan himself indicates this when he states: "The great initial thrust for efficiency and economy against a young weak profession in the years after 1911 started the unfortunate developments in educational administration and fifty years of inadequate support of our public schools has continued to extend their influence." The current leader of the accountability movement, Leon Lessinger, is a practicing school administrator with experience as a school superintendent, U.S. Office of Education official, professor of educational administration, and dean of a school of education. It seems, then, that educational administrators are part of the problem.

In both our historical examples, opposition came from teachers; the more organized the teachers, the more effective the opposition. Given the present highly organized state of teachers in this country, it seems reasonable to conclude that they will be the group most likely to combat accountability. Recall that the teacher opposition in our historical examples had both an economic and an educational aspect: the former being a matter of job protection and salary, the latter a result of teachers having first-hand experience with the consequences of an emasculated curriculum. If our analysis is correct, the solution to the problem will first have to stress the political and economic roots, since these are the basic issues involved. The educational issues will have to be put aside temporarily, but they soon will resurface.

Economically speaking, the fiscal crisis as exemplified by accountability presents a formidable challenge to teacher organizations. First, existing economic arrangements seem stacked against teachers and other state employees. Given the state support of corporate capital, the inequitable tax structure, and the taxpayer revolt, teachers are faced with a public which is undoubtedly responsive to the accountabilists' cries for less waste and more efficiency in the public sector. For the first time, teachers will have to address themselves directly to the issues of how the funds for salaries and supplies are to be raised. The regressive tax structure will have to be analyzed, publicized, and countered with alternatives so the public can see the economic distribution of wealth in the society. If, as the social scientists argue, the private enterprise–government merger represents a mixing of previously separate political and economic realms in the higher circles of society, politics and economics will have to merge in the programs of teachers and other nonmembers of these circles. Extending the strategy of combining economic demands with the political programs to carry them out, O'Connor specifies that the only long-range solution for public employees is an alliance with their clients. Until this alliance takes place, teachers will continue feeling the economic pressure of accountability movements.

Any call for an alliance between teachers and their clients, the parents of the students, must be detailed. Why and how should the alliance come about? This is certainly not an easy union to achieve since economically, at least in the short run, the interests of tax-paid teachers and tax-paying parents conflict. Yet, if the results of recent Gallup polls are accurate, teachers have a certain reservoir of good will on which to build such an alliance. Overlan (1973) discusses the results of Gallup polls for the years 1969–1972 and concludes that there is a solid base of support for public education among "almost all American parents." The article states that when parents are asked to report what they consider particularly good about the public schools, their first response is, "the teachers." Yet this should not provoke any great sense of ease among teachers, since the poll also indicates that parents report finances as the number one school problem. Our recommendation for specifying sources for funds sought should constitute a reasonable first step in attempting to deal with the issue of school expenditures.

Achieving a teacher-parent alliance in the nation's great urban centers may be somewhat more challenging. The support shown in a national poll may well be weaker in the cities than in the suburbs. The school achievement differentials between students in city systems and those in suburban systems would indicate urban parents have less to be thankful for from their schools. Also, the ethnic and class differences between urban teachers and urban parents are larger and more difficult to bridge than those in the suburbs. Yet the urban school systems are undoubtedly where the impact of accountability and the fiscal crisis is being and will be felt most. Any political and economic alliance between urban teachers and urban parents would have to begin with the educational concern that links these two groups: the welfare of urban children. Yet, if we look closely at how educational policy is made in urban schools, we find that teachers have little if any input into the process. If a meaningful alliance is to be achieved, teachers must first obtain a significant role in educational policy making and policy implementation in urban schools.

We have briefly indicated two strategies through which teacher organizations can deal with the accountability threat: (1) specification of tax-raising methods in seeking funds for educational expenditures, and (2) moves to obtain control over educational matters in the urban school systems. More concretely, teacher organizations, as they bargain collectively, will have to include the fund raising and budgeting process in the negotiations and will have to begin to bargain on the educational issues of curriculum, instructional methods and technology, evaluation criteria for teachers and students, and school-community relations.

The prospects of teacher organizations' implementing these strategies are less than bright, because this kind of bargaining would deviate from the traditional view of the tasks of teacher organizations. Teacher organizations, both unions and associations, share the orientation to their tasks of most American labor which has been

termed *business unionism.*[8] The organizations tend to
devote themselves to the salaries, wages, and working
conditions of their members. Activities which are not
directly related to tangible economic benefits are not
stressed. Political activity is undertaken by a business
union only in pursuit of economic gain. The suggestions
made above should be considered not so' much an indict-
ment of present-day policies as an indication that the
policies need updating to deal with current conditions.

Yet the strategies of teacher organizations have been
shifting away from business unionism, as can be seen in
the increased political activity of both of the national
teacher organizations and their affiliates.[9] Nevertheless,
the strategies suggested above would create further
changes in the organizations' activities: changes which
emphasize educational issues at the local level by including them in the bargaining process, and changes
which would make the political programs of the organizations broader than rewarding friends of education
and punishing enemies at the polls.

We can find relatively concrete models for implementing the strategies called for in this chapter by again con-
sidering the historical evidence. History, besides show-
ing us that issues which occur in the present have parallels in the past, also can provide students of the present

[8] On business unionism, see Samuel P. Hays, *The Response to
Industrialism* (Chicago: University of Chicago Press, 1957), 64.

[9] The American Federation of Teachers is affiliated with the
American Federation of Labor–Congress of Industrial Organizations and participates with the AFL-CIO in its Committee on
Political Education (COPE), the affiliate of that organization
which undertakes political activity. The National Education Association (NEA) has recently joined with two municipal unions
in activity similar to that of COPE.

with a range of alternative institutions and strategies which, although they may have failed in the past, still have something fresh to say about modern problems. We offer two such historical alternatives.

G. D. H. Cole (1920), early in the twentieth century, developed a social theory which advocated that society be organized through a collection of guilds. Cole's plan involved all parts of society, and he recommended that production workers be organized into self-governing guilds. One of the evils which Cole sought to overcome through the guilds was the system of payment by results, which, although it had been abolished in education, had managed to maintain itself in industry. Cole's recommendations for reorganizing the educational system are instructive. "We need, then, in . . . our educational system . . . , an Educational Guild, in which the teachers will possess a self-governing status fully equivalent to that of economic workers. . . ." He goes on to say that the Educational Guild would have to be organized on both national and local levels, self-government would have to exist in both the individual school and at the level of national policy making, and the Educational Guild of self-governing teachers would have to be prepared to negotiate with representative councils of local parents and other interested citizens. The relationships among the groups just mentioned and many other organized groups discussed by Cole are complex. Yet his analysis shows that such a plan is theoretically possible and worthy of consideration by contemporary teachers.

Cole's advocacy of a teacher-governed school negotiating with organized groups of parents is far from the reality of American urban education. Yet an institution did exist in American urban education that at least partially anticipated the teacher-governed school. Many American urban school systems had active teachers' councils during the late nineteenth and early twentieth centuries (Ortman, 1923). These councils were composed of groups of teachers who advised the superintendent and board of education on how educational policies would affect the teachers and students. The existence of these councils during the same era and in the same locations as the "cult of efficiency" in school administration suggests that at least one alternative might have existed to that movement. The councils, however, were only advisory; and they never became the potent vehicles for a teacher voice that they might have been.

Yet teachers' councils, or something like them, might well provide a vehicle for teacher input in modern school management. Of course, the councils would have to be more than advisory. If teacher organizations are to include management concerns in their bargaining, they could do so effectively by negotiating for teachers' councils in each local school and also at the district and system levels. These councils would concentrate on educational policy, while the other organizations of teachers would continue exercising their economic and political functions.

A teaching profession organized (1) into bodies which would be politically active in seeking economic reforms to fund the schools equitably, and (2) into councils which sought self-government of the schools by the teachers—that teaching profession would be in a position to work with organized parents. Since the fiscal crisis is greatest in the large urban systems, we can understand why citizens in urban centers are beginning to organize over more and more issues. Organized teachers and organized parents would provide a structure in which the groups with the most to gain from public schooling would have the most powerful influence on the institution. Perhaps even some kind of meaningful Parent-Teacher Association would evolve in place of the farcical and manipulative institution currently paid lip service by both parents and teachers.

The set of institutions described herein, or something like it in which both teachers and parents have a real voice in education, would lead to a genuine system of political accountability of educational groups to each other. It would replace the economically biased, budget-cutting, elite-serving accountability which is the current reality and the current threat to American public education.

REFERENCES

Ayres, Leonard P. 1909. *Laggards in the Schools.* New York: Macmillan.

Callahan, Raymond E. 1962. *Education and the Cult of Efficiency.* Chicago: University of Chicago Press.

Cole, G. D. H. 1920. *Guild Socialism: A Plan for Economic Democracy.* New York: Frederick A. Stokes.

Coltham, Jeanette B. 1972. Educational Accountability: An English Experiment and its Outcome. *School Review.* LXXXI: November, 15–36.

Doll, William E. 1972. A Methodology of Experience: An Alternative to Behavioral Objectives. *Educational Theory.* XXII: Summer.

Glass, Gene V. 1972. The Many Faces of Educational Accountability. *Phi Delta Kappan.* LIII: June, 636–639.

Hays, Samuel P. 1957. *The Response to Industrialism.* Chicago: University of Chicago Press.

Hofstadter, Richard. 1955. *The Age of Reform: From Bryan to F.D.R.* New York: Vintage.

Lessinger, Leon M. 1970. *Every Kid a Winner: Accountability in Education.* Palo Alto, Cal.: Science Research Associates.

Levit, Martin. 1972. The Ideology of Accountability in Schooling. *Educational Studies.* III: Fall, 133–140.

Marland, Sidney P., Jr. 1972. Accountability in Education. *Teachers College Record.* LXXIII: February, 339–345.

Mills, C. Wright. 1956. *The Power Elite.* New York: Oxford University Press.

O'Connor, James. 1970. The Fiscal Crisis of the State. *Socialist Revolution.* No. 1, January–February, 12–54; and No. 2, March–April, 39–94.

Olmsted, Richard. 1972. Review of *Every Kid a Winner. Harvard Educational Review.* XLII: August, 425–429.

Ornstein, Allan C., and Harriet Talmage. 1973. The Rhetoric and the Realities of Accountability. *Today's Education.* LXII: September–October, 70–80.

Ortman, Elmer J. 1923. *Teacher Councils: The Organized Means for Securing the Cooperation of All Workers in the School.* Montpelier, Vermont: Capital City Press.

Overlan, Francis S. 1973. Our Public School Monopoly. *New Republic.* September, 14–18.

Perkinson, Henry J. 1968. *The Imperfect Panacea: American Faith in Education, 1865–1965.* New York: Random House.

Simon, Brian. 1960. *Studies in the History of Education, 1780–1870.* London: Lawrence and Wishart.

Small, Alan A. 1972. Accountability in Victorian England. *Phi Delta Kappan.* LIII: March, 438–439.
Urban, Wayne J. 1973. Teachers, Politics, and Progressivism: The Early Years of Atlanta Public School Teachers Association. Unpublished paper presented to the History of Education Society, Chicago, Illinois.

IV

The Economics and Politics of Accountability

In the twentieth century the bureaucratic structure has increasingly dominated public school administration. It has effectively excluded public school teachers from the important educational concerns of professional, curricular, and fiscal policy decision making. Even with the current growth of union strength, teachers generally have not gained meaningful control over the processes of their work; in fact, they have been ever more dominated by a rigid hierarchical bureaucracy.

The accountability movement in American education, we believe, greatly threatens newly acquired teacher power by preventing teachers from gaining control over educational policy decisions affecting their work. It might be argued that "teacher surplus" is a greater threat than accountability, but we suggest that this "surplus" is more a creation of policy making than a reality. Most teachers seeking employment are needed and could be usefully absorbed in the educational system provided proper political and economic reforms were made. It is not a historical accident that "teacher surplus" and accountability in education surfaced just when teachers began to make significant economic gains through their collective efforts. But the convergence of these three important historical developments is a complex issue that will require extensive research and analysis.

Nevertheless, when more research has been completed, we suspect that accountability will be seen as a means to stabilizing the teacher labor market by selecting out and firing teachers. This process serves a three-fold purpose not only for astute administrators but also for the corporate system as a whole. On the one hand, it assuages the angry inner-city parents who feel their children are getting inferior schooling; it leads these parents to believe something significant is being done for "equal opportunity." At the same time, it reinforces the image of the teacher as the problem and, by using the teachers as scapegoats, continues to divert attention from the real sources of the problem of inequality. Finally, it provides a stabilizing barrier to effective class-consciousness by teachers while claiming objectivity, fairness, and universality of standards. In this way accountability can be used to stall the growing power of teacher unionism, and to further constrain schools from becoming sources of individual self-discovery for both students and teachers. We think accountability is the most effective means thus far for distracting teachers and getting them to capitulate to a deadening form of positivistic learning.

IMPORTANCE OF BUREAUCRATIC LANGUAGE

Those teachers first encountering accountability terminology must have been bewildered by the complexity of a bureaucratic language which was used to explain the myriad of educational benefits. Claims by proponents of this movement vary widely as to what can be achieved: from what amounts to a basic 3 R's curriculum to a humanistic one or from the claim of centralized to decentralized control of the schools. It seems as though the language is created first, and theory and practice are subsequently considered and then rationalized. In any case, teachers are confronted with the deadening task of learning a new lexicon of terminology and symbols. Management by objectives, systems analysis, inputs, quality control, educational engineering, vouchers, generic and enabling objectives, activities and competencies, omnicompetencies, modules, CBTE, PBTE—these are the more salient linguistic drudgery that the neophyte to accountability faces.

Of course, slogans are not unique to today's teachers. They have had a long history of spurious influence in our schools. Nevertheless, educational slogans seem to have added a special significance for the present accountability movement. As Israel Scheffler (1960) posits, educational slogans "make no claim to facilitating communication or reflecting meaning," but are

> repeated warmly and reassuringly rather than pondered gravely. . . . They provide rallying symbols of the key ideas and attitudes of an educational movement. They both express and foster community of spirit, attracting new adherents and providing reassurance and strength to veterans. . . . With the passage of time, however, slogans are often increasingly interpreted . . . as literal doctrines or argument, rather than merely as rallying symbols. When this happens in a given case, it becomes important to evaluate the slogan both as a straightforward assertion and as a symbol of a practical social movement.

A linguistic analysis of the slogans used in the accountability movement is, of course, not possible here, but it does seem necessary to note the important, and sometimes critical, role they and their ideological implications play in the movement. Over and over again one reads and hears "business/management/efficiency" and "science of education" language. In even a cursory examination of the movement, the economic implications and purposes become obvious in the very nature and the structure of accountability language.[1]

THE ECONOMICS OF ACCOUNTABILITY

Theoretical Basis

The search for a broad theoretical rationale for the contemporary accountability movement can be found in the behavioristic/mechanistic theories of B. F. Skinner, but more "practical" theories began with the initial writings of the high priest of the movement, Leon Lessinger. In his pioneering work, Lessinger (1970) compared the American educational system to a malfunctioning machine and emphasized the necessity of preparing "educational engineers" to correct that malfunction. His industrial model of the teacher as an educational engineer called for a "workable technology of instruction" and "certain managerial procedures that both stimulate the demand for performance and help to provide it." The educational engineer provides "tables and text" on how much it will cost the community

---

[1] For an extended discussion of the relationship of slogans to accountability, see Margaret Linsey, "Performance-based Teacher Education: Examination of a Slogan," *The Journal of Teacher Education,* Vol. XXIV, No. 3, Fall 1973, 180–186.

for performance contracting. Continuing, Lessinger declared that

> A major objective of educational engineering is to arm educational practitioners with both the technological competence of essential engineering generalizations, strategies, and tools and the professional practice of a successful instructor or educational manager.

Lessinger and a number of other accountability spokesmen seem intent upon equating the functions and purposes of schools to business and industry, and they seem obsessed with the economics of schooling. Speaking from an organizational, managerial, and technological point of view, Lessinger compared formal education to a "cottage industry."

> Costs accelerate, yet there is little improvement in productivity. The "industry" is labor intensive—over 85 percent of the average budget is spent for salaries and for benefits related to salaries. Such a share of the educational dollar, coupled with teacher militancy, collective bargaining and tenure, presents such community problems of runaway costs divorced from responsive improvement.

Lessinger's warnings about the growing threat of "powerful" teacher unions to school budgets had to strike a responsive note among cost-conscious school administrators, parents, and politicians. Yet he continued to proclaim humanistic objectives while judging the success of our schools in purely economic terms.

Cost Accounting in the Schools

James G. Abert (1974) [2] has blatantly and unequivocally advocated cost-cutting in the schools. Abert maintains that the financial problems facing the schools should cause educators to "look at education as an industry and start to speak of the effects of shifting such ratios as capital for labor and out-put to labor" (that is, schools must shift from being labor-intensive industries to capital-intensive industries). Education is considered as an enterprise whose employees compete for a share of the national product with employees in all areas of the economic activity. To prevent teacher wage deterioration relative to industrial employees Abert suggests two possible remedies to school officials.

> The first is to follow the lead of manufacturing industries . . . . by substituting capital for labor [automation], thus increasing the capital-to-labor ratio [educational hardware, cheaper than teachers]. The second is to vary the labor mix systematically such that while the range of wages, high to low, may not change, larger numbers of employees are at the low end, thereby holding the average wage down. [3]

Noting what he considered a rapid increase in wages for elementary and secondary schools, Abert then emphasizes that

[2] Former Director of Research, National Center for Resource Recovery, and Deputy Assistant for Evaluation and Program Monitoring at HEW.

[3] What this would do, at least for a while, would be to throw teachers into the "secondary" labor market.

It is important . . . not to lose sight of the fact that there must be fewer hands [teachers] . . . The labor force mix strategy requires . . . "cheaper" people to be mixed with the trained professional cadre. There are [three] obvious groups who can and do provide services at less than the prices demanded by regular employees [teachers]. . . . Students . . . retirees . . . and volunteer or semi-volunteer housewives . . . It would seem obvious that large shifts to student instruction—call it supervised peer groups or peer group plus-a-couple-of-years . . . might pay handsome dividends. The same is true of using large numbers of retiree paraprofessionals in the classroom.

In fact, Abert's "experimental" proposals are already being carried out in nearly all school districts. Consider the cutting of services and staff and the hiring practice of employing the beginning teacher, paraprofessionals, and permanent substitutes who are less experienced but much cheaper than the experienced teacher. Also, today all types of educational hardware are used. There is independent and group study, programmed instructional materials, team teaching, peer-group—instructional assistance, and many other teaching/learning cost-cutting techniques. Written materials favoring accountability are laden with promises of economic efficiencies for school systems that implement competency or performance-based educational programs. The ideas flowing from such literature not only buttress present cost-accounting practices in the schools but provide the theoretical basis for the future proliferation of these practices and for many yet-to-be developed ones that are on accountability drawing boards.

Teachers Victimized

Teachers cannot help but become the most victimized party in such economic considerations. Their increased economic vulnerability will in turn lead to greater alienation. They become alienated from the process of their work since, as professionals, they sell their labor for use in a mechanistic system in which they have little real power or autonomy. And by extending this analogy between the schools and the economic behavioral basis of the modern firm, we see the student becoming even more blatantly the merchandisable product. It is not difficult to see that accountability contributes to the development of individual identities as market commodities.

Even those educational strategies in the accountability mold which allegedly concentrate on each individual student are, in reality, marketing procedures which manipulate the student into developing harmony with both macro- and microorganizational demands. Thus, while the controls will be of a "soft" scientific nature, they still attempt to control both students and teachers.

In short, more boundaries and more complexities overload the already ponderous bureaucratic system, and change becomes all the more difficult to contemplate, let alone effect.

Influence of Peter Drucker

The most sophisticated economic justification for accountability, we believe, comes not from the pen of an education scholar but from the writings of Peter Drucker, the highly regarded dean of American management science. In his book, *Management,* Drucker (1974) declares that service institutions, like schools, must stop being such parasites on the well-being of the market economy; that is, all service institutions, such as schools, are paid for from economic surplus and, therefore, they are social overhead. But it is not just the increasing cost of service institutions (schools) that makes it mandatory for them to be managed. Schools are mismanaged and are justifiably attacked for lack of performance. In fact, says Drucker, schools must look to business to learn management by objectives; at present, they simply are not managed. We must, he continues, make school work productive and the workers (teachers) achieve. Managing schools for performance—holding them accountable —is our greatest managerial need today. Schools need not differ from the firm, and indeed really are not different except for terminology. Differences are in technology, not substance.

For Drucker, the major difference between schools and business is that schools must be based on effectiveness, not efficiency. Effectiveness (student achievement) can be measured easily and precisely by the use of behavioral objectives. Indeed, achievement is never possible except if it is measured against specific, limited, clearly defined targets. Performance must no longer be the ability to increase one's budget, as has too long been the case with schools. Schools have gotten away with substituting public relations for performance. Drucker terms teachers *knowledge workers* and claims they must be managed like any other workers. But what really matters is for schools to be accountable and truly to focus on results.

To summarize, Drucker believes the schools need:

1. Clear objectives and goals
2. Priorities of concentration

3. Measurements of performance
4. Feedback and to build in self-control from results
5. Organized audit of objectives and results
6. Identification of unsatisfactory performance and activities that are obsolete, unproductive, or both
7. Abandonment of low-performance activities
8. Competition between schools to hold them to performance standards.

And for those who may not see any seriousness of purpose or urgency in Drucker's proaccountability message, he declares, "We cannot tolerate the present system much longer—we must hold schools to rigorous performance standards."

THE POLITICS OF ACCOUNTABILITY

Accountability is critically interwoven not only with the economics but also with the polity of the corporate state. National politicians have spoken in support of education accountability. Congressman Roman Pucinski of Chicago, for example, referred to educational engineering as a coming revolution in America. Indeed, the majority of the state legislatures have mandated competency-based teacher education programs. Performance contracts between government and private corporations have developed in the early 1970s: HEW with the Rand Corporation and the OEO's $5.6 million investment in 18 school districts, to name a few.

Teacher Unions

Teacher unions have also become involved in the politics of accountability. Under the title of "accountability," the preamble to the contract between the New York City Board of Education and the United Federation of Teachers (UFT) for the period September, 1969 to September, 1972 pledged that the union and the board would "develop objective criteria of accountability."

This statement was in part an outgrowth of the political struggles over community control in some New York City schools in the late 1960s, especially the Ocean Hill–Brownsville Schools. UFT President Albert Shanker (1973) asserted that an accountability system would give teachers the greatest protection ever known by guarding competent teachers from unwarranted criticism and providing assistance to less capable teachers.

But Shanker did not view accountability as parents did. Parents (mainly black) wanted teacher accountability to ensure a better education for their children; whereas Shanker, although desiring quality education, gave priority to better teacher protection. This placed Shanker's position on accountability outside the sphere of pedagogical matters and into the arena of the politics of teacher power (*vis-à-vis* black parents). He was especially concerned about the possible erosion of teacher power resulting from accountability schemes. The political struggle between black parents and Shanker (and the UFT) resulted, in part, from varying interpretations of accountability.

National Politics

Support for accountability came even from the very highest office in the land. As early as 1970, President Nixon, in a special message to Congress on educational reform, stated his backing for the movement. Attacking the high cost of "failure" of federal compensatory education programs, he compared federal money spent to the poor results in achievement.

> From these considerations we derive another new concept: accountability. School administrators and school teachers alike are responsible for their performances and it is in their interest as well as in the interests of their pupils that they be held responsible . . . We have, as a nation, too long avoided thinking of the productivity of the schools.

In this same message Nixon called for the establishment of the National Institute of Education which was soon to be given a leading role in spearheading many accountability schemes.

Soon after being appointed by Nixon to the high post of United States Commissioner of Education, Sidney P. Marland, Jr. (1972) began championing the cause of accountability. He proclaimed, "I laud such elements of accountability as are present in performance contracting . . ." and viewed "management by objectives . . . as an important key to the smooth operation of our contemporary education institution." Describing in great detail his pride and commitment to the widespread use of accountability within the U.S. Office of Education, Marland lauded efforts to establish management objectives but warned that this was

> . . . the very first and relatively modest step in the management by objectives process. Once large objectives have been hammered out, each must be broken into specific and carefully defined subobjectives. Accountability is implicit from day to

day and from month to month as all echelons in the
Office of Education focus their energies on the
objective and its sub-objectives and perform the
various tasks which lead to their completion.[4]

Calling for a "science of evaluation," Marland specu-
lated (frighteningly so, to us) on the future of accountability.

Indeed, within our time—perhaps within the next
ten years—there could well be a nationwide accounting process or institution which would act like a
certified public accountant in business, objectively
assessing the success and failure of our schools and
reporting the findings to the public. . . . How pro-
ductively are our teachers being used . . . is the
professor using his time and talents in such a way
as to change the lives of his students—and how
many? These are pertinent questions of accountability and as our schools and colleges face economic
crisis, the questions become even more crucial.

His concern with the application of business/efficiency
management technology to an increased teacher productivity clearly placed Marland in the ideological camp

[4] For a unique account of centralization-decentralization theory
of public organizations, see Herbert Kaufman's article, "Administration Decentralization and Political Power," *Public Administration Review*, XXIV: 1, January–February, 1969, 3–15. For an
almost wholly descriptive look at what we like to call the "revolv-
ing, reformist administrative shell game," note what Kaufman
views as the cyclical nature of the politics of public administration,
which can "roll with the punches" or "scores an early knockout,"
but still stays in control of the fight.

of those political figures favoring the political and economic uses of accountability.

State Politics

M. M. Gubser (1972), Dean of the College of Education at the University of Arizona, describes one of the
more open displays of accountability's being used to
indoctrinate students into right-wing political and economic ideas. The Arizona Board appointed "basic goals
commissions" which set goals to be used as criteria for
statewide selection of texts and supplementary books
and for deletion of offensive and controversial passages
in instructional materials. To make certain teachers did
not deviate from the goals and behavioral objectives of
the state-mandated curriculum, the state board of education approved a performance recertification based on
performance testing.

Through these techniques, the board attacked political and academic freedom under a smokescreen of accountability. Gubser predicted

It may be the beginning of a national trend.
California's Governor, Ronald Reagan, in a recent
address, cited Arizona's developing educational situation as a model for his and other states. The nation-
ally syndicated ultraconservative radio program,
Lifeline, sponsored by oil millionaire H. L. Hunt,
has urged school patrons throughout the country
to press for legislation and curriculum patterned
after that adopted in Arizona. In Georgia a situation
remarkably similar to Arizona's has developed over
the past year. Texas (and numerous other states) has
now legislated performance-based teacher education
and criterion-referenced instruction.

We fully share Gubser's concerns and fear the possibility of other forms of sociopolitical oppression under the guise of accountability.

There are numerous and diverse examples of the economic and political uses of the accountability movement in education. Accountability advocates—from the President of the United States to the local politician or businessman—are often fiscal conservatives not known for their support of progressive social legislation. These men are far more interested in maintaining the status quo than in initiating change. But some politicians and administrators of a more liberal persuasion are also among the ranks of those pushing accountability, and the success or failure of the movement depends, we believe, upon the future support or opposition of these liberals. They are cognizant of the benefits derived from the socioeconomic stability promised by accountability, and they often become the leading spokesmen for an essentially conservative movement.

REFERENCES

Abert, James G. 1974. Wanted: Experiments in Reducing the Cost of Education. *Phi Delta Kappan.* V:444–445.

Drucker, Peter. 1974. *Management.* New York: Harper & Row.

Gubser, M. M. 1973. Accountability as a Smokescreen for Political Indoctrination. *Phi Delta Kappan.* LV:64–65.

Kaufman, Herbert. 1969. Administration Decentralization and Political Power. *Public Administration Review.* XXIV:1:3–15.

Landers, Jacob. 1973. Accountability and Progress by Nomenclature, Old Ideas in New Bottles. *Phi Delta Kappan.* LIV:539.

Lessinger, Leon M. 1970. *Every Kid a Winner: Accountability in Education.* Palo Alto, Cal. Science Research Associates.

Linsey, Margaret. 1973. Performance-Based Teacher Education: Examination of a Slogan. *The Journal of Teacher Education.* XXIV:3:180–186.

Marland, Sidney P., Jr. 1972. Accountability in Education. *Teachers College Record.* LXXIII:344.

Morgart, Robert, Gregory Mihalik, and Don Martin. 1973. Can/Should the Schools Change the Social Order? The Problem of the Professional Proletariat —The American Public School Teacher in the 1970's. Unpublished paper presented to The American Educational Studies Association. Denver, Colo.

Nixon, Richard M. 1970. Excerpts from the President's Special Message to Congress on Education. Excerpted in the *New York Times.* March 4, 28.

Scheffler, Israel. 1960. *The Language of Education.* Springfield, Ill.: Charles C Thomas.

Shanker, Albert. 1973. Accountability: The Hazard of Blame-Placing. *New York Times.* January 7, 95.

V

The Conclusion

Our examination of the accountability movement has led us to conclude that it is not an educational but rather a political movement fueled by economic concerns. Economic and political forces provide the main thrust behind the movement that has attracted many who really believe that it will improve education. These forces aim to hold down costs at all levels of education while at the same time striving to maintain the economic and political status quo, complete with all its present inequities.

Accountabilists know that the easiest way to reduce educational costs is to pare down the highest and most rapidly accelerating cost of education: teacher salaries. Accountability is a vehicle well designed for such a task. Government officials, legislators, school boards, and administrators recognize this weapon. Consequently, many of them embrace accountability as an idea whose time has come.

But accountability involves far more than the reduction of educational costs. It is also well designed to combat the rising collective power of teachers and to prevent them from moving toward any degree of real self-management. Conversely, collective action which achieves a significant degree of self-management may well be the best—and possibly the only—way for teachers to extricate themselves from their present state of alienation.

Proponents of accountability also laud the "quality control" aspects of the movement. But we are convinced that expanding hierarchical bureaucratization is incompatible with quality work. The refinement, improvement, and introduction of quality control schemes into schools will only serve to further alienate teachers from their work and thus lower the quality of their work. According to Richard Goodwin (1966):

> . . . a truly rigorous system of quality control in an organizational structure as exists in most public education, would assume the dimensions of a subordinate bureaucracy which would add the deficiencies of that form to the (already existing) incapacities . . .

The accountability movement attempts to apply mechanical solutions to a complex social institution. It constitutes an emerging power scheme designed to prespecify goals that are usually simplistic, irrelevant to the learner's developmental process and environment, inhibiting to his potential, empirically unverifiable, and logically indefensible. These prespecified goals function mainly to control what teachers will do in the classroom, and, even more important, to control the overall economic and political affairs of the school. The spokesmen for the movement often allege that everyone involved in the educational process should have a hand in formulating goals. But this promise looks, in the light of our investigation, very much like a diversionary tactic intended to give teachers and parents a false sense of control over the educational decision-making process. The higher echelons of authority will ultimately make the important economic, political, and educational decisions that affect schools.

Accountability favors a hierarchy even more rigid than that which already exists in the schools. Its widespread implementation is increasingly likely to alienate teachers. Although teachers will be given the opportunity to develop and implement goals for students, administrators will do the same for teachers, and so on up the line all the way to state and perhaps eventually to federal levels. Teachers will be given freedom only within very strictly predefined limits. Under such circumstances, school systems will resemble large corporations where each subordinate is held directly accountable to his immediate superior at every rung of the hierarchical ladder. But the locus of real control will remain at the top, the locus of accountability at the bottom.

Leading advocates of accountability, such as Leon Lessinger, attempt through their writings to convert teachers into technocrats by requiring those teachers to give priority to a restless pursuit of efficiency and productivity. Such a pursuit, however, can take on all the trappings of what Richard Goodwin (1966) has termed a modern "scientific mysticism":

> The rational pursuit of a mystical idea is not rational, however, and if it is carried far enough, it loses whatever reason it once claimed . . . [whenever] scientific reason expands its claim of authority to include the social process and is then carried to its logical conclusion, scientific reason becomes a form of secular mysticism.

Accountability has at its core a secular mystique which emphasizes economy, modernization, and extreme systemization. Teachers must be burdened with rigid techniques, "objective" data, and measurable evaluation procedures. All this leads, we suggest, to an increasing fragmentation of knowledge. Education becomes no more than a servant to the economic production process. If successfully implemented; accountability would bring only an oppressive system of control for teachers; it would intensify their alienation from their work.

But our concern is not confined to teachers. What of students in an age of accountability? In particular, what of those students who are inclined to ponder, meditate, and reflect?

Students who ponder, meditate, and reflect have no place in an accountability classroom. They would not be doing what they ought. As Stuart Hampshire (1970) has put it:

> In fact, reflections, meditations, pondering are what is typically going on in the minds of persons who are not fully employed in some specific task or performance. Reflection and meditation may be just the things that we do contrast with performing . . . . The important philosophical point, it seems to me, is that we all recognize this kind, or if you like, sense of the word "thinking," the reflecting, pondering, meditating one, which typically has no immediate consequences in behavior, no generally invariable effects of a behavioral kind.

In an accountabilist classroom, the kind of thinking that educators have so often in the past referred to as "reflective" must be replaced by "adaptive behavior."

If judgments about the success of instructional processes are to be made exclusively on the basis of prespecified changes in learner behavior, and if the teacher is to cleave solely to objectives framed in terms of measurable learner behavior, as James Popham (1972) recommended, then no other conclusion seems possible. By this definition, a student who is just sitting and thinking is engaging in no measurable form of learning. Therefore, he is doing nothing relevant to the educational process. And if his thinking results in behavior incompatible with the objectives which have been prespecified, then he must be stopped. The teacher's responsibility in such a situation would be to interrupt this thinker, to call him back to his appointed task of the moment, and to get him (literally) moving again. Only at their own risk could teachers tolerate, let alone encourage, this pondering and reflecting. In full knowledge that salary, promotion, and professional prestige all depend directly on the extent to which their students accomplish prespecified behavioral objectives, teachers could hardly avoid regarding thinkers as threats to their own personal well-being. But what kind of educational scheme is it that renders the emergence and development of reflective thinking so inimical to the interests of teachers? What kind of education is it which puts teachers under such pressure to oppose the development of children's critical faculties?

The accountabilist pedagogy cannot be equated with the concept of education. It is not education. It is, rather, indoctrination dictated by modern educational technology. And there is reason to believe that it could turn out to be very effective. If we were to make our schools into arenas of constant "busyness," in which there was no time or opportunity to "stop and think" and only punishments (or perhaps carefully planned schedules of behavior modification) awaiting those who try, we might well suppress the development of critical faculties in our students.

As Stuart Hampshire has said, "It seems almost impossible that I could meditate or ponder in the middle of a football scrimmage." The experience of one of the authors with competency-based modules in teacher education, which he has taught, indicates that the module is a very fitting analogy to Hampshire's football scrimmage. If carefully planned, zealously administered, and buttressed by the advantages of modern behavior modification techniques to ensure that the recalcitrant remain constantly at their tasks, modular scheduling might well suppress all critical or creative thought in the schools.

The ultimate effect of accountability schemes, if they were to become sufficiently entrenched in the schools, would be to prevent not only teachers but also students and eventually "accountabilist trained" adults from taking collective action in their own behalf. The sharing of mutual meanings and concerns would become increasingly difficult as the distinction between rational social action and adaptive behavior blurred. Indeed, only the adaptive behavior would be stressed. As Trent Schroyer (1971) concluded:

> . . . the greatest problem that social theory faces is not whether behaviorism, game theory, or systems analysis is theoretically valid, but whether it might not become valid through a self-fulfilling prophecy justified by a technocratic ideology.

If this reformulation of education took place, the future of science itself would be in jeopardy. A closed system of knowledge would result. And that upon which both the integrity and the autonomy of science depend—its capacity to be self-critical and self-correcting—would be lost. Scientists, like accountabilists, would necessarily lean toward instrumental interpretation of all situations. Without the tool of critical thinking, they would have to rationalize and justify their activities by reference to the instrumentally viable. Their methodology would become a politicized form of induction. It would emphasize only observation of data with an eye toward discovering recurrent physical and social regularities toward the ultimate end of social control. Reference to alternate theoretical considerations—be they ethical, political, epistemological, or even scientific—would disappear, as technologically oriented practitioners of science grew increasingly reluctant to give them serious consideration. In the training of such technologically oriented scientists, accountabilist schools could, and presumably would, make an important contribution.

Finally, the authors do not believe that the accountability movement will result in significant economies. A proliferating bureaucracy buttressed by special needs for independent auditing and evaluation could well generate new careers and new payrolls. In such a case, the monetary costs would most likely turn out to be even higher than they are now. But even if a system of accountability could lower or hold the line on educational expenditures, there are costs other than the monetary which should be considered. The question, of course, is whether an education which is both cheap and sound can be achieved. If we are to have any confidence in historical precedent, the answer to that question seems to be clearly in the negative.

However, nothing we have said is intended to claim

that accountability proposals are always inappropriate. In the last analysis, they all result in techniques intended to modify a specific behavior in a specific way which can then be evaluated quantitatively. For such purposes, the techniques which constitute the heart and soul of the accountability movement are appropriate. And there is evidence that they work fairly well. The problem lies in the attempt to broaden the assumptions underlying these techniques in such a way as to constitute a "philosophy of education" for the entire educational process. For accountabilist techniques are techniques of indoctrination. To adopt them wholesale is to replace education with a variety of forms of indoctrination and that is a bad bargain. The cost is too high and it is one that our children will have to pay. In the words of Paul Feyerabend (1970), any method that encourages conformity, be it empirical or not:

. . . is in the last resort a method of deception. It enforces an enlightened conformism and speaks of truth, it leads to a deterioration of intellectual capabilities, of the power of imagination, and speaks of deep insight; it destroys the most precious gift of the young, their tremendous power of imagination, and speaks of education.

REFERENCES

Feyerabend, Paul K. 1970. How to be a Good Empiricist- A Plea for Tolerance in Matters Epistemological, from *Philosophy of Science: The Delaware Seminar II.* Reprinted by permission of the University of Delaware Press in Baruch A. Brody, *Readings in the Philosophy of Science.* Englewood Cliffs, N.J.: Prentice-Hall, Inc., 333.

Goodwin, Richard N. 1966. *Triumph or Tragedy: Reflections on Vietnam.* New York: Random House.

Hampshire, Stuart. 1970. A Peculiar Kind of Thinking, in *Mind Science and History.* Howard E. Kietar and Milton K. Munitz, editors. Albany, N.Y.: State University of New York Press, 53–58.

Morgart, Robert, Gregory Mihalik, and Don Martin. 1973. Can/Should the Schools Change the Social Order? The Problem of the Professional Proletariat—The American Public School Teacher in the 1970's. Unpublished paper presented to The American Educational Studies Association. Denver, Colo.

Popham, James W. 1972. Focus on Outcomes: A Guiding Theme of E.S. '70 Schools, in Olson and Richardson, editors. *Accountability: Curricular Applications.* Scranton, Pa. Intext Publishers.

Schroyer, Trent. 1971. The Critical Theory of Late Capitalism, in *The Revival of American Socialism.* George Fischer, editor. New York: Oxford University Press, 299.

Wilson, Elizabeth C. 1971. Quality Control in the Public Schools. *Educational Technology.* October, 25–29.